Typhoon

Group Captain Denys Edgar Gillam
DSO, DFC, AFC, DL

Battle of Britain

The Photographic Kaleidoscope

VOLUME II

Battle of Britain

The Photographic Kaleidoscope

VOLUME II

Dilip Sarkar

Ramrod Publications

Other books by Dilip Sarkar: -

SPITFIRE SQUADRON: *19 Squadron at War, 1939-41.*
THE INVISIBLE THREAD: *A Spitfire's Tale.*
THROUGH PERIL TO THE STARS
ANGRIFF WESTLAND
A FEW OF THE MANY

BADER'S TANGMERE SPITFIRES: *The Untold Story, 1941.*
BADER'S DUXFORD FIGHTERS: *The Big Wing Controversy.*
MISSING IN ACTION: *Resting in Peace?*
GUARDS VC: *Blitzkrieg 1940.*
BATTLE OF BRITAIN: *The Photographic Kaleidoscope*

Dilip continues to collate Battle of Britain related information and photographs. **BATTLE OF BRITAIN:** *The Photographic Kaleidoscope* **VOLUME III** will be released in September 2000. Dedicated to members past and present of the Battle of Britain Fighter Association and with a Foreword by Air Commodore Peter Brothers, this work is likely to represent the largest collection of hitherto unpublished photographs made available since 1980.

His future titles will include further *Kaleidoscopes* and **JOHNNIE'S KENLEY SPITFIRES,** concerning Wing Commander JE Johnson's leadership of the Canadian Wing, which has been researched over a number of years and will soon be complete. A new and unique Douglas Bader related book is also under review.

Concurrently with this book, Ramrod Publications has released **BATTLE OF BRITAIN:** *The Movie* (ISBN: 0-9519832-9-6), a profusely illustrated and fascinating book concerning the epic film by 'FlyPast' Assistant Editor Robert Rudhall. For further information on Ramrod titles and our unique inter-active promotional events, please contact Anita at the address given below.

BATTLE OF BRITAIN: *The Photographic Kaleidoscope* **VOLUME II**   ISBN: 0-9519832-8-8   © Dilip Sarkar 2000

First published 2000 by Ramrod Publications, 16 Kingfisher Close, St Peter's, Worcester WR5 3RY. Tel: 01905 767735, fax: 01905 424533, e-mail: *anita@ramrodbooks.u-net.com.*

Designed and typeset by Ramrod Publications. Printed in UK by Aspect Print & Design, 89 Newtown Road, Malvern, Worcs WR14 2PD.

Dedication

This book is dedicated to the one man responsible for ensuring the survival of the British people in 1940, the Air Officer-Commander-in-Chief of RAF Fighter Command: -

Lord Dowding, First Baron of Bentley Priory

Acknowledgements

Firstly I must thank Odette, Lady Dowding for so kindly supporting my work and contributing the Foreword to this title.

I must also thank my father, Mr TC Sarkar JP, for taking me to watch the Battle of Britain film when I was eight-years old; had he not done so I doubt that any of my books would ever have arisen.

Grateful thanks are also extended to all friends who have contributed photographs to my collection throughout the last 20 years. Likewise without them this series of publications would be impossible.

As ever I must make specific mention of two particularly close friends and supporters: Andrew Long who does a great job copying old photographs often at short notice and whose help in other ways remains immeasurable, and the poet Larry McHale whose enthusiasm is an inspiration.

Last but not least, my wife Anita whose industry, ability and sound business sense I have relied upon more over the years than ever she realises.

Contents

Foreword

Dilip Sarkar first contacted me back in 1996 when he was writing the much acclaimed Bader's Duxford Fighters: The Big Wing Controversy. Having happily contributed information and photographs towards his research, it gave me great pleasure to join Dilip and his charming wife, Anita, at the book's launch, which took place at Worcester Guildhall in September 1997. It was delightful to meet there many foramer Battle of Britain pilots and various support personnel, and equally so to discover the level of interest that the summer of 1940 continues to generate – thanks in no small part to the efforts of Dilip Sarkar himself, his friends and supporters. To them I must, in the first instance, say 'well done'.

As the late First Lord Dowding, the Commander-in-Chief of RAF Fighter Command in 1940, was my father-in-law the Battle of Britain will always hold a particular fascination for me personally. Furthermore, my late husband, Derek, the Second Lord Dowding was himself a Spitfire pilot in 1940. It was not always easy for him, I know, having his father as Commander-in-Chief, but between them the Dowdings certainly played their part in Britain's Darkest Hour.

It was a travesty that my father-in-law was not made a Marshal of the Royal Air Force in recognition of his great victory, but it is nevertheless appropriate that we can now see his statue outside the 'RAF church' in London. The bronze was unveiled by HM the Queen Mother, wartime Queen of England, this being not only a moving moment for my husband but also all of those present who brought about this marvellous tribute.

Dilip Sarkar rightly points out that the name of Hugh Dowding remains largely unheard of by people today. I am grateful to him, therefore, for dedicating this fascinating book in memory of my late father-in-law and admire enormously Dilip's praiseworthy efforts to publish so much Battle of Britain history that would otherwise have gone unrecorded.

The Right Hon. Odette, Lady Dowding
London, January 2000.

Author's Introduction

Sixty years ago, on May 10th, 1940, Nazi Germany invaded the west. Just 25 days later, the British Expeditionary Force, having fought a bloody fighting withdrawal across Belgium and northern France, was evacuated from the beaches of Dunkirk. Three weeks later France surrendered, the ominous swastika already flying over Poland, Norway, Denmark, Holland, Belgium and Luxembourg.

As America steadfastly pursued its foreign policy of Isolationism from events in Europe, Britain stood alone. The unprecedented advance to the Channel provided the unexpected opportunity for Germany to consider mounting a seaborne invasion of Great Britain. Despite the shocking collapse of the west and America's continued neutrality, Britain refused to negotiate terms with Herr Hitler. Rallied by their Prime Minister, Winston Churchill, the British people resolved to fight on, regardless of the odds.

Between July 10th and October 31st, 1940, the 'Battle of Britain' was fought over England as the *Luftwaffe* attempted to wrest aerial supremacy from the RAF as a prelude to a seaborne invasion. It failed. The might of the apparently all-conquering Nazi war machine had been defied and beaten by the aircrew of RAF Fighter Command, 544 of which, often fighting against overwhelming odds, lost their lives in the process. This 'Agincourt of the skies' remains a tremendous inspiration.

Over the years my personal research has been undertaken almost exclusively through primary sources, in particular concerning recording survivors' memories and biographies of casualties. During this process I have collected many photographs, the majority snapshots from private collections. Thus my books have never relied upon the widely used RAF and IWM collections, available to all, but have been profusely illustrated with these unique windows through which we can still catch a glimpse of 1940.

My research has always been balanced, it is fair to say, with all due accord and attention also being given to the *Luftwaffe*. An interesting point arising, however, is that private RAF Battle of Britain photographs are much rarer than the German equivalent. The Germans, it seems, were obsessed with photography. Whilst researching *Guards VC: Blitzkrieg* 1940 (Ramrod Publications, 1999), concerning the Fall of France, I was amazed to discover the quantity available of such photographs taken by German soldiers. On every unit there seemed to be an unofficial photographer who funded his hobby through selling snaps to his comrades. The same is true of the *Luftwaffe*. Many German veterans have, therefore, extensive photographic collections that provide superb records of their wartime experiences.

It was a different story on our side of the Channel, however. Former Spitfire test pilot Jeffrey Quill, himself a Battle of Britain airman, once said to me 'in 1940 our minds were not focussed upon posterity!' A common response to requests for photographs from members of 'Churchill's Few' is, in fact and to quote in particular Wing Commander 'Red' Stavert: 'Photography on military installations was, of course, restricted, and in any case film was in short supply. It was not something we considered to any degree, and in any case we had more pressing things to worry about in 1940!' Nevertheless, and fortunately for us today, Allied personnel did take, in fact, a surprising number of unofficial photographs in 1940. Having spent many years in search of and collecting such material with a view to eventual publication, it now gives me great pleasure to present some of these gems in this unique series of books.

The original, and highly successful, *Battle of Britain: The Photographic Kaleidoscope* (Ramrod Publications, 1999), was actually intended to stand alone. However the combination of an apparently insatiable demand for such a production, coupled with the enormity of my personal archive dictated an early decision: not to re-print but continue to produce further volumes, based upon the original concept, until such time as suitable material becomes exhausted.

Battle of Britain photographs have always held a particular fascination for enthusiasts and historians alike, myself included. Surprisingly however, the crop of pilots' autobiographical accounts published in the 30 years or so after the war are all, without exception, extremely lacking in photographic material. Why publishers should have adopted this formula is puzzling when, as I now know, the personal albums of the authors are frequently impressive. For me personally the small number of photographs in each book was always a great frustration, so the opportunity to present such books as this gives me great pleasure. In this way countless photographs from private collections will be published that might otherwise never see the light of day. That in itself totally justifies the effort of all involved, as reflected by Steve Beebee's review of the original *Kaleidoscope* on *www.amazon.co.uk:* -

Imagine you were a fly on the wall at squadron airfields during the Battle of Britain. This book offers an unorthodox insight into the characters and events of the times. The pictures included are not stylised or posed, and were not – in most cases – taken for official purposes. This lends them a much more authentic air than many of the stiffly posed pictures of the time.

With that I would not disagree, and in fact, given the comparative rarity of RAF Fighter Command related photographs, we have concentrated exclusively on that subject in this volume (although plan a dedicated *Luftwaffe Kaleidoscope* for the future).

The emphasis of all *Kaleidoscope* photographs, reflecting my own interest, is in the human element of the Battle of Britain. The only criterion in the photographs' selection is that they are interesting (although most could be considered rare), in terms of either the actual image or story relating. From my viewpoint each volume also provides an excellent opportunity to sometimes revisit and update accounts from my previous works. This formula is, we at Ramrod believe, a new concept and we thoroughly enjoy putting these rather special publications together.

Volume III, in fact, is already in production and scheduled for release in September 2000. With a Foreword by Battle of Britain pilot Air Commodore Peter Brothers, this book will probably be the largest collection of previously unpublished photographs released for 20 years. Personally I can't wait to see it!

The Foreword of the first *Kaleidoscope* was contributed by our great friend and supporter Lady Bader, and it is an equal honour and privilege that Odette, Lady Dowding has so kindly written the Foreword to this, Volume II. Beyond any doubt, Air Chief Marshal Sir Hugh CT Dowding, the true architect of victory in the Battle of Britain, was not only shamefully treated afterwards by the authorities, but has since largely been forgotten. Indeed, as one of 'Dowding's Chicks', Flight Lieutenant Wallace Cunningham DFC once said to me: -

Lord Dowding is the big success story – a strong man who had resisted political pressure to throw away a lot more fighters in France for a battle already lost. He was preserving Fighter Command for the battle to come. Victory in the Battle of Britain was down to him. Clearly his was the credit for the strategy. He listened, said little but acted decisively. I had direct experience of his quick and clear thinking when our 20 mm cannons were performing badly; he visited us of 19 Squadron and within hours we were re-equipping with machine-gun armed Spitfires. So treasure the memory of 'Stuffy' Dowding – do not sell him short. His was the victory in directing and sustaining his 'Twelve Legions of Angels'.

Incredibly, for reasons far too complex to cover here (but see my Bader's Duxford Fighters: The Big Wing Controversy, Ramrod Publications, 1997), Dowding was not made a Marshal of the RAF. The service has argued that MRAF is reserved for those who have been Chief of the Air Staff (CAS), but I would respectfully point out that neither MRAF Lord Douglas of Kirtleside or MRAF Sir Arthur Harris ever served in that exalted appointment. Nevertheless, in 1943, Air Chief Marshal Dowding received a hereditary peerage, appropriately becoming the First Baron of Bentley Priory. In 1970, Lord Dowding died at his home in Tonbridge Wells. Group Captain Douglas Bader is on record as having said at that sad time: -

Lord Dowding is probably unknown to most of the younger generation. Yet it was because of him as much as any other man that they have been brought up in the English way of life, speaking the English language. They might have been speaking German. Without his vision, his planning, his singleness of purpose, and his complete disregard for personal aggrandisement, Fighter Command might have been unable to win the Battle of Britain in the summer of 1940. What rankled most with the fighter pilots of 1940 was that he was never made MRAF. Seldom in our history has a man deserved so much of his fellow countrymen but wanted and received so little. He surely earned his place alongside Nelson and Wellington and other great military names in our history.

Thirty years later what Group Captain Bader said still holds true: Lord Dowding remains largely anonymous, especially to the younger generations – many of whom, it must be said, have never heard of the Battle of Britain or even the great Douglas Bader himself. We can only hope that with the 60th anniversary of the Battle of Britain now upon us, the story of Lord Dowding and Fighter Command's victory in 1940 will be brought to the attention of a wider audience. If this book helps achieve that, then our efforts have been justified.

Dilip Sarkar.
Worcester, England, New Year's Day 2000.

Hugh Caswall Tremenheere Dowding pictured early on between the wars and soon after being commissioned into the RAF. During the Great War Dowding had been a fighter pilot and leader, an experience later to serve him well. In 1916, however, he had quarrelled with his GOC, Major-General Trenchard, who forbade pilots to wear parachutes believing them to be 'bad for morale'. This was the start of a catalogue of incidents between Dowding and the Service that would all eventually contribute towards his downfall in 1940. In 1930, Dowding became the Air Member for Supply and Research, arguably from which point onwards he began preparing for the Battle of Britain. Opposing the prevailing belief that 'the bomber will always get through', his view was that the 'security of base is an essential pre-requisite'. It is Dowding we have to thank, in fact, for the Hurricane and Spitfire, not to mention the far-sighted integration of radar into the country's air defences. In 1936, Air Marshal Dowding became the first Air Officer Commander-in-Chief of RAF Fighter Command. Being already familiar with both the new fighters and radar, he was the perfect choice. Significantly his SASO was Air Commodore Keith Park, a Great War fighter 'ace' from New Zealand, in whom Dowding found the perfect right-hand man. Fortunately for all concerned, by 1940 Air Vice-Marshal Park was commanding No 11 Group, defending London and the southeast.

Air Chief Marshal Dowding's HQ Fighter Command was located at Bentley Priory (Stanmore in Middlesex) where on September 6th, he received the King and Queen. Although an oft used photograph from a series taken during that visit, it is still of interest; I wonder what the Air Chief  Marshal is thinking? His office, the Dowding Room, is preserved, in fact, and appropriately the Battle of Britain Fighter Association enjoys an annual reunion at Bentley Priory for which occasion I was personally honoured to join 'Churchill's Few' in 1997.

Although not made MRAF, ACM Sir Hugh Dowding did become the 1st Baron of Bentley Priory, a hereditary peerage. After his death in 1970, Lord Dowding was appropriately buried in Westminster Abbey where this simple marker can be found in the Battle of Britain Chapel.

Other memorials to 'Stuffy' include, of course, the superb bronze statue outside the 'RAF Church' of St Clement Dane in London. Somewhat lesser known is this tribute at Moffat, his place of birth. Appropriately the plaque records Lord Dowding as a commander, strategist and humanitarian. Some argue today that Lord Dowding should be made a posthumous MRAF; personally I doubt that the authorities would ever comply, as doing so would be an admission of guilt regarding Dowding's shocking treatment after his great victory.

Instrumental in bringing about the downfall of both Dowding and Park, following the so-called 'Big Wing Controversy', was the ambitious and influential Air Vice-Marshal Trafford Leigh-Mallory. Never a fighter pilot himself, nevertheless in 1940 'LM' commanded No 12 Group, protecting the industrial Midlands and the north. Here he is pictured (centre) at a party in late 1940 with Spitfire pilots of 609 'West Riding' Squadron. At second and fifth left are Flying Officers David Crook DFC and Michael Appleby.

The legless Squadron Leader Douglas Bader commanded No 242 Squadron in 'LM's' 12 Group. He believed that instead of merely awaiting an assistance call from 11 Group and then being used largely to protect AVM  Park's airfields whilst his fighters were in action, 12 Group should in any case sally forth in numbers to attack and destroy the enemy *en masse*. Today the record shows that this idea was, in fact, fundamentally flawed and totally contrary to Dowding's carefully considered 'System' (that was actually working perfectly). Nevertheless 'LM' and other officers of Air rank, none of whom had the fighter experience of either Dowding or Park, supported the idea and used the tactical controversy as a tool for personal advancement. So it was that Leigh-Mallory would later succeed Park as AOC of the prestigious 11 Group, whilst ACM Sholto-Douglas replaced Dowding.

Amongst Squadron Leader Bader's young Hurricane pilots was Pilot Officer Denis Crowley-Milling. An 'Old Malvernian' and former Rolls-Royce apprentice, 'Crow' was in awe of his swashbuckling leader. Their friendship was only terminated by the death of Group Captain Bader in 1982. 'DCM' was then instrumental in founding the Douglas Bader Foundation (information regarding which can be found elsewhere in this book) to provide a facility for amputees at Roehampton and uphold 'DB' as an example to the disabled. Sadly Sir Denis himself died in 1996, but the Foundations work continues. He is pictured here in 1942 whilst one of the first Hawker Typhoon Wing Leaders.

Operating out of Duxford, Squadron Leader Bader led three 12 Group fighter squadrons into action for the first time on September 7th, 1940, on which day the Germans began heavily bombing London. The Hurricane of Pilot Officer Crowley-Milling (P3715, LE-H and not 'M' as often reported, pilot's personal flying logbook refers) was damaged in the radiator in combat over the Thames Estuary. With his armoured glass windscreen shattered by a cannon shell, 'Crow' made a successful forced-landing at Stow Maries.

When Squadron Leader Bader was appointed to command, the pilots of No 242 Squadron were essentially experienced Canadian flyers whose morale was poor following a battering during the Battle of France. Outspoken amongst
them was Pilot Officer Percival Stanley Turner. 'Stan', as he was widely known, became 'DB's' right-hand man and
in 1941 would command 145 Squadron in Bader's legendary Tangmere Wing. Turner later flew with distinction over
the Middle East, where he is pictured here, and survived the war with the DSO and a DFC and Bar to his credit.
Turner and Crowley-Milling, in fact, were amongst a small number of Bader friends and supporters actually men-
tioned by name in the famous Danny Angel film 'Reach for the Sky'.

Without a doubt the place to be for any ambitious career officer in 1940 was at the head of a fighter squadron. Consequently many pre-war regular officers were brought from outside Fighter Command to fill such appointments, amongst them Squadron Leader Phillip 'Tommy' Pinkham AFC. A Chief Flying Instructor posted to command No 19 Squadron at Duxford on June 5th, 1940, exactly three months later he was dead, shot down over Kent in what was his first engagement. Here Pinkham (centre) is pictured whilst flying biplane Bulldog fighters with No 17 Squadron in 1937. Although 'Monty' sadly perished that same year, I wonder who was 'Michael' and, indeed, what became of him?

Before the war, Squadron Leader Pinkham had also flown Gauntlets with the RAF Meteorological Flight, collating vital data for the weathermen. Here he is pictured aloft on such a sortie. It is shocking to think that we could so easily have gone to war in such obsolete machines.

My personal 'hero of heroes': Squadron Leader Brian Lane DFC. After Pinkham's death in action, to 19 Squadron's delight 'Chiefy' was officially given command. After Squadron Leader Stephenson was lost over

Dunkirk on May 26th, Lane had, in fact, led the Squadron in the air and largely continued to do so even after Squadron Leader Pinkham's arrival (the latter being preoccupied with the troublesome experimental cannon). Described as a 'quiet, compelling leader' Lane was rightly awarded the DFC for his good leadership of the Squadron during Operation DYNAMO.

A snapshot taken from the personal album of Flight Lieutenant Wallace Cunningham DFC showing himself (extreme left) with 'Flash', the German Shepherd and Squadron Mascot owned by Flight Sergeant George 'Grumpy' Unwin DFM, and Squadron Leader Brian Lane DFC; the other pilot is unknown.

Taken on the same day at Fowlmere Farm, Duxford's nearby satellite airfield that played host to the Sector's Spitfire squadrons, Flight Lieutenant Cunningham demonstrates an alternative way of wearing a service cap. The Spitfire is a Mk IIA, P7849, 'QV-J', 'Armagh: the Belfast Telegraph Spitfire'.

Pilot Officer Wallace Cunningham (left) chatting outside the pilot's hut at Fowlmere with Pilot Officer Eric Burgoyne. The latter's death in action on September 27th, 1940, dates this picture as shortly before then. Of interest is Cunningham's 'VR' lapel insignia and undone top button – the sign of a fighter pilot. Also, in common with photographs of other 19 Squadron pilots around this time, Burgoyne is wearing what appears to be a khaki battledress top.

A fascinating and poignant photograph from the personal album of Wing Commander David Cox DFC, in 1940 a humble RAFVR Sergeant Pilot on 19 Squadron. This snapshot of the Squadron returning from a sortie in late September was taken by Sergeant Cox himself. Although the trees appear bare, as David points out (the caption is contemporary and his own hand) '1940 was a very hot summer indeed'. The 11 Spitfires are flying in a most unusual formation suggesting that an aircraft is perhaps missing.

CHIEFY J AEROPLANE.

Another snapshot from Wing Commander Cox's album, this time showing the personal Spitfire of Squadron Leader Brian Lane DFC (note rank pennant beneath cockpit). Of great interest are the highly irregular rear-view mirrors fitted externally either side of the armoured windscreen. 19 Squadron veterans recall with amusement a 'wingless' Air Commodore's visit who insisted that Lane should remove these non-regulation mirrors. Our hero's response: "Well you fly the bloody thing then – Sir!"

From the personal album of Flight Lieutenant Richard Jones, a Pilot Officer serving in both 64 and 19 Squadrons during 1940, comes this superb snapshot study of the Czech Pilot Officer Frantizek Hradil at Fowlmere during summer 1940. 'Haddy' was shot down and killed by *Hauptmann* Rolf Pingel over Southend on November 5th, 1940.

Another Czech serving with 19 Squadron was Pilot Officer Frantizek Dolezal, posing here with the same Spitfire Mk IIA as in the previous photograph (note angle of propeller). Tragically although 'Dolly' survived the war a Wing Commander with the DFC to his credit, he was killed in a flying accident in Czechoslovakia in October 1945.

Harry Walpole Charnock, at 35-years, was much older than most fighter pilots during 1940. He had been a pre-war NCO pilot cashiered for a low-flying misdemeanour in 1930. In 1939, however, trained service pilots like Charnock (and indeed the legless Douglas Bader) were in demand, hence his return to active service. Previously flying with 64 Squadron, Charnock arrived at 19 Squadron in October 1940, scoring several successes between then and completion of his tour in 1941, which saw him awarded the DFM. Having enjoyed further success over the Middle East, Flight Lieutenant HW Charnock DFC DFM was demobbed in 1945 and died in 1974.

The pre-war RAF Volunteer Reserve provided not only the opportunity for fit and intelligent young men to learn to fly at His Majesty's expense, but also, as was intended, a vital reserve of trained service pilots. Many of these pilots were called up in August and September 1939, thereafter either concluding their formal service flying training or being posted to operational units. This is Arthur Vokes, a VR pilot from Edgbaston in Birmingham, pictured by his civilian-flying instructor, a Mr Langley, at Sywell Airfield in Northamptonshire shortly before the outbreak of war. By June 1940, Pilot Officer Vokes was flying Spitfires with 19 Squadron and was 'combat ready' in time for the Battle of Britain, which he survived with some success.

As Fighter Command geared up for the 'Non-Stop Offensive' of 1941, the character and composition of its squadrons changed as veterans were rested and casualties were replaced. By August 1941, for example, 19 was commanded by Squadron Leader Walter 'Farmer' Lawson DFC, his two flight commanders being Flight Lieutenants Wallace Cunningham and Arthur Vokes. This photograph was taken that month at Itteringham Mill and shows Vokes (centre) with two post-Battle of Britain pilots, Pilot Officers Devereux and Buchan.

August 28th, 1941, was a black day for 19 Squadron which saw Squadron Leader Lawson killed in action and Flight Lieutenant Cunningham captured during an escort sortie to bombers attacking enemy shipping off the Dutch coast. The following day, Flight Lieutenant Vokes, now the Acting CO, led what was left of the Squadron on an ASR sortie over the North Sea. Unfortunately the Spitfires ran into a number of Me 110s from 6/ZG76. Four of 19 Squadron's pilots failed to return. A week later, on September 5th, Vokes himself was dead, having crashed in bad weather near Langham aerodrome on a ferry flight. This is his original grave marker, at Great Bircham, Norfolk, pictured on the day of his funeral.

The Service Plot of the cemetery at Great Bircham on the occasion of HM the King, George VI, unveiling the Cross of Sacrifice on July 14th, 1945. The parents of Flight Lieutenant Vokes, along with other loved ones of the fallen buried here, were sent

this photograph at the King's suggestion in 1946. One wreath was laid by HM the Queen, the others on behalf of RAF Bircham Newton.

Best wishes to Dilip and the Malvern Spitfire Team.

Noel MacGregor
Sgt/Pilot 19 Sqdn.

Alexander Noel MacGregor was a NCO VR pilot posted to 19 Squadron in September 1940. Here he is pictured at Fowlmere in 1941 with a Spitfire Mk IIB. Note the 'chocks' and 1941 'escape' pattern flying boots, the fur lined uppers of which were detachable to give the boot the appearance of a civilian shoe, a useful ruse in the event of the pilot being shot down over enemy occupied territory.

Although Spitfires *still* look up-to-date, so pleasing to the eye and forward thinking was RJ Mitchell's inspirational design, the transport used in 1940 often has a more primitive appearance! Here 19 Squadron's Czech pilots go three-up: Pilot Officers Dolezal, Plzak and Hradil, Fowlmere Farm, summer 1940.

The officers of 19 Squadron pictured outside their Mess at Folwmere in June 1941. The occasion is the leaving 'do' of their popular Commanding Officer, Squadron Leader Brian Lane DFC (right). Sadly Lane was shot down and killed over the North Sea on December 13th, 1942. The victim of 6/JG1's *Oberleutnant* Walter Leonhardt, Lane is commemorated on both the Pinner War Memorial and the Runnymede Memorial to 'Missing' Commonwealth aircrew. The author of the classic first-hand account *Spitfire!*, Lane was doubtless destined for great things but remains a comparatively unsung hero of our Finest Hour.

Flight Lieutenant Lawson clay pigeon shooting at Fowlmere. Shooting either clays or game was a great means of gunnery practice popular with many fighter pilots.

Jack Lawson tries his hand at 'piloting' a petrol bowser whilst Arthur Vokes climbs aboard.

More light relief at Fowlmere: Squadron Leader Lawson at the reins whilst Pilot Officer Cowley hitches a ride (early summer 1941).

A jovial looking Air Commodore James Coward AFC pictured on a visit to England from his Australian home in 1990. On August 31st, 1940, Flying Officer Coward of 19 Squadron was shot down in Spitfire X4231, the first to enjoy the benefits of both machine-gun and cannon armament. Fortunately Coward baled out but during the descent had to stem severe bleeding from his left leg by applying a tourniquet made from his flying helmet's earphone wire. Although his leg was amputated, he returned to active flying duties.

Flying Officer Coward landed by parachute near the Royston-Newmarket Road, his Spitfire impacting nearby. Years later the crash site was excavated by Richard Payne who recovered, amongst other things, this rather historic Hispano-Suiza 20mm cannon. A cannon shell from this aircraft is in my collection uncommonly dated '1939'.

Credit: Roger Miller

Someone who can vividly recall the bombing of Fowlmere that day is former 19 Squadron Flight Rigger LAC John Milne. A 'Halton Brat', John recalls his Battle of Britain experiences with enthusiasm and is a popular guest at our events.

Fowlmere Farm, near the IWM Duxford Airfield in Cambridgeshire, as it appears today. If ever there was a place to walk with ghosts…

Credit: Andrew Long

Groundstaff of the Czech 310 Squadron at Duxford in 1940. At right is Bill Kirk, then an Orderly Clerk now a popular guest at our book signings.

Some 57 years later, Bill Kirk finds himself on the right of another line-up, this time at Ramrod Publications' Battle of Britain Symposium held at Huntingdon Hall, Worcester, in March 1997. Also pictured are Battle of Britain pilots Flight Lieutenants Ken Wilkinson and Gordon Batt, and 66 Squadron aero-engineer Bob Morris.

Ken Wilkinson, from Cheltenham, was another VR pilot who completed his *ab intio* flying training at Staverton in Gloucestershire. After serving with 19 Squadron during 1940, Ken became an instructor before flying sweeps with 165 Squadron. Here he is pictured with his Spitfire Mk IX in 1943.

An excellent Duxford study of a Battle of Britain Hawker Hurricane of the Czech 310 Squadron: P3148, 'NN'Q'. Of interest is the covered slit-trench intended to afford some protection to groundcrews caught out in the open in the event of an air raid. From Bill Kirk's personal album.

Provided by Croydon enthusiast Colin Brown (via Piper), this has to be amongst the most evocative Battle of Britain photographs I have ever seen. The snap was taken at Croydon in September 1940, showing Hurricane L2012 of 605 Squadron. On September 15th – Battle of Britain Day – Pilot Officer TPM Cooper-Slipper 'rammed' (his description) a Do 17 of 5/KG3 over Marden. Fortunately the young pilot landed safely by parachute and was only slightly injured. The vehicle is a petrol bowser, the very real threat of enemy attack indicated by the wearing of steel helmets.

Although the VR provided a reserve of trained pilots ready for call up at a moments notice, the Royal Auxiliary Air Force provided what were in effect 'territorial' squadrons that were fully staffed in every respect. Until general mobilisation in September 1939, however, many personnel were still part-timers. Auxiliary aircrew were largely from affluent backgrounds, many of which already flew for pleasure at weekends and soon developed a flamboyant reputation. This classic period studio portrait is of an Auxiliary pilot, Flight Lieutenant Richard Hellyer of 616 'South Yorkshire' Squadron of the RAAF.

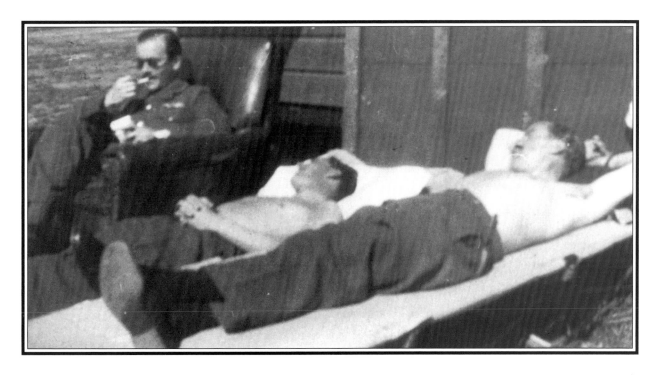

Apart from a brief interlude in June 1940 when the Squadron participated in Operation DYNAMO and flew from Rochford, between October 1939-August 1940 the Spitfire-equipped 616 Squadron operated from Leconfield in 12 Group. In this slightly out of focus snapshot taken there during the summer of 1940, three 'South Yorkshire' pilots relax at dispersal; left to right: Flight Lieutenant Richard Hellyer, Pilot Officer Donald Smith and Flight Lieutenant Teddy St Aubyn. During the Squadron's hectic time at Kenley in August, St Aubyn was shot down and wounded. Smith was killed on September 27th when 616 was a component of the so-called Duxford Wing. Hellyer survived the war but is now buried with his wife and youngest son at Tangmere Church. He is survived by his eldest son, Richard, who successfully organised the 'Tangmere 99' reunion weekend in order to raise funds for the church roof.

Another Leconfield snap: Flight Lieutenant St Aubyn is seen here in conversation with a non-flying Squadron Leader who, from his medal ribbons, appears to be a Great War veteran. Sadly St Aubyn was killed flying Mustangs in 1943.

The rather dashing, 20-year old Flight Lieutenant Colin MacFie. Another Auxiliary member of 616 Squadron, at the height of the Battle of Britain MacFie was transferred to become a flight commander on 611, another Auxiliary Spitfire squadron serving in 12 Group. Unfortunately

he was amongst the many experienced pilots lost by Fighter Command during offensive operations over France in 1941. Captured in July, MacFie served in the post war RAF before finally retiring in 1963. He is believed to have died in reduced circumstances during 1982.

In a posed shot believed taken at Kirton-in-Lindsey during late 1940, at centre is an original 616 Squadron Auxiliary, Flight Lieutenant Ken Holden. A squarely built and forthright Yorkshireman, Holden would later become a leading light in Wing Commander Bader's Tangmere Wing as the CO of 610 Squadron. Like fellow 616 Auxiliary Lionel 'Buck' Casson, he later became a post-war CO of the 'South Yorkshire' Squadron.

Another original member of 616 Squadron was Hugh 'Cocky' Dundas, who, according to his friend Air Vice-Marshal JE Johnson, appeared to be 'related to have the aristocracy in northern England!' Dundas became a successful fighter pilot, and later leader, to whom we can credit the 'Finger Four' formation (based upon the highly successful *Luftwaffe Schwarm*, worked out by Wing Commander Bader and Flying Officer Dundas at Tangmere in 1941). A long-time friend and supporter of mine, Group Captain Sir Hugh Dundas died in 1996.

Howard Frizelle Burton was a regular RAF officer and product of the Staff College at Cranwell (where he won the Sword of Honour in 1936). A successful Spitfire pilot with 66 Squadron during the Dunkirk fighting, in September 1940 he became CO of 616, leading that Squadron onwards into 1941 and throughout the Tangmere Wing period. Later successful over the Middle East, 'Billy' Burton was amongst a number of highly decorated Battle of Britain pilots shot down off the Bay of Biscay whilst returning to North Africa after a conference in 1943. He remains 'Missing'. He is snapped here in with Tommy gun in 'gung-ho' pose at Westhampnett in 1941. He is wearing a highly prized German *Schwimmveste*.

The widow of Group Captain HF Burton DSO, DFC & Bar, Mrs Jean Allom, poses with his sheepskin Irvin flying jacket in 1996. In 1999, a joint presentation of Burton memorabilia, including the 1936 Sword of Honour, was made to RAF Cranwell by Mrs Allom and relatives of her late brother-in-law (the Group Captain's brother).

Having suffered heavy losses at Kenley, 616 Squadron was withdrawn to Kirton-in-Lindsey in 12 Group where it became a 'C' Squadron, receiving and providing extra training for new replacement pilots. Amongst these was none other than Pilot Officer JE 'Johnnie' Johnson, a VR pilot destined to become the RAF's top scoring fighter pilot in World War Two. 'Johnnie' is pictured here at left during the winter of 1940.

In 1990, impressive celebrations took place in London to mark the Battle of Britain's 50th anniversary. This group of former 616 Squadron personnel is pictured about to enter the grounds of Buckingham Palace. Pilots present are Group Captain Sir Hugh 'Cocky' Dundas (second left, back row), Group Captain Denys 'Kill'em' Gillam (third left, back row) and Squadron Leader Lionel 'Buck' Casson (second from right). Sadly both Dundas and Gillam have since died.

An early Hawker Hurricane of No 11 Group's 56 Squadron based at North Weald in Essex. Fortunately by the Battle of Britain the original fixed pitch airscrew had been replaced, first by the improved variable pitch De Havilland then Rotol propeller. The ability to alter pitch is vital given that the effect is akin to changing gear in a car.

A pre-war regular commissioned pilot with 56 Squadron, Flying Officer Percy Stevenson Weaver from Chippenham, Wiltshire. Note the white pre-war flying suit.

A pre-war group of white overalled 56 Squadron pilots at North Weald. Weaver is pictured second right. A very successful fighter pilot during the Battle of Britain, notification of Weaver's DFC arrived on August 31st, 1940. Sadly 'Mouse' would never learn of this himself as he failed to return from a fierce combat over the River Blackwater. Although his body was never found, Flight Lieutenant Weaver's name is commemorated on the Runnymede Memorial.

More 56 Squadron pilots, this time undertaking some DIY car maintenance at North Weald; who are they please?

Spitfire Pilot: Flying Officer David Crook DFC of 609 'West Riding' Squadron. Well-known as the author of the excellent first-hand account *Spitfire Pilot*, published in 1942, Crook also wrote the lesser-known wartime thriller *In Pursuit of Passey*.

In the RAF, unlike the *Luftwaffe*, fighter pilots were rested after a certain period and temporarily transferred to other duties, generally instructing, ferry or test flying. Although a successful pilot in 1940, Crook became an instructor soon afterwards but did not return to a fighter squadron. Here he is pictured at right, as a Flight Lieutenant bearing the DFC ribbon, with an unknown fellow instructor. The aircraft is a Miles Magister, used for initial monoplane dual experience.

Another excellent photograph of David Crook, wearing Irvin jacket in front of another 'Maggie'. Sadly his PRU Spitfire crashed into the sea off Aberdeen in 1944, as a consequence of which he has no known grave.

Unlike most young fighter pilots, David Crook was married. This is his wife, Dorothy, more commonly known as 'D', by which pet name she is referred to in *Spitfire Pilot*. (below)

In 1990 I traced 'D', now Mrs Hessling, to her Birmingham home and was astonished to discover that, by sheer coincidence, the Hesslings had known my parents during the 1960s! I remain most grateful to Dorothy for so kindly contributing much material towards my research, including a copy of 'DMC's' original *Spitfire Pilot* manuscript.

An early research project was the history of Spitfire R6644 that crashed near Malvern in 1941 (see my *The Invisible Thread: A Spitfire's Tale*, Ramrod Publications 1992). This work entailed identifying and tracing this aircraft's pilots, amongst whom I discovered was Air Vice-Marshal FDS Scott-Malden. During the early summer of 1940, R6644 had been on charge with 5 Operational Training Unit at Aston Down, near Stroud in Gloucestershire, and it was there that the fledgling fighter pilot, Pilot Officer David Scott-Malden, soared aloft just once in this particular machine. He was to become not only a highly successful fighter pilot and Wing Leader but also one of the youngest Group Captains in the Service.

In 1992, I had the great pleasure of meeting Air Vice-Marshal Scott-Malden, to whom I was able to present a mounted piece of Spitfire R6644 (recovered by the Malvern Spitfire Team in 1987). Sadly the Air Vice-Marshal died shortly before publication of this book.

Another senior RAF officer it was my pleasure to meet was Air Commodore HW 'Tubby' Mermagen. Another Cranwellian, and like Douglas Bader a famous pre-war aerobatic pilot, during the Dunkirk fighting and early part of the Battle of Britain he commanded 222 Squadron. After a brief spell as CO of 266, another Spitfire unit, he later served in the Middle East and in a host of senior staff appointments. Pictured here whilst serving in Berlin during 1945, the Air Commodore sadly died in 1997, aged 85.

A 504 'City of Nottingham' Squadron Hurricane on finals, Filton, near Bristol, in September 1940. Having already been heavily engaged whilst flying from Hendon, after the successful and surprise KG55 raid against Filton on September 25th, 504 was posted to that airfield the following day. When KG55 returned to the West Country on September 27th, 504 was amongst the Fighter Command squadrons that fell upon the raiders and inflicted significant losses.

Credit: Allan White

504 Squadron's Sergeant Ray Holmes pictured with his groundcrew at Filton. He would later become famous for ramming the Do 17 that consequently fell on Victoria Station, September 15th, 1940.

Credit: Allan White

504 was another Auxiliary Squadron, which perhaps explains the sports car's presence here at Filton. The pilot is Flying Officer MEA Royce whose brother, Flight Lieutenant WB Royce, served in the same Squadron. Both survived the war. As a matter of interest, the black flying suit was another affectation of pre-war pilots!

Credit: Allan White

504 Squadron's Sergeant Charlton 'Wag' Haw pictured in Scotland before the Battle of Britain. Haw was amongst the pilots from this Squadron who later flew with the Russians. A successful pilot, Haw survived the war to leave the RAF in 1951 as a Squadron Leader with a DFC to his credit.

Flying Officer John Hardacre, from Birmingham, was a regular RAF officer who flew with 504 Squadron during both the Battles of France and Britain. Another successful fighter pilot, Hardacre's Hurricane was shot down in combat over the West Country on September 30th, 1940. His body was washed ashore 10 days later and the 24-year old lies buried at All Saint's, Fawley, Hampshire.

Credit: Allan White

Although the markings indicate that this 504 Squadron mishap occurred after the Battle of Britain, this Hurricane, V6732, was on charge with the unit during the Battle of Britain. This incident occurred at Exeter early in 1941.

Credit: Allan White

Amongst the NCO VR pilots serving with 504 Squadron in 1940, was Basil Martin Bush. Better known as 'Mike', he was later commissioned and also went to Russia. Back in the UK he became an instructor at Shobdon in Herefordshire and later flew Mosquito bombers with 139 Squadron at Upwood. Here Flight Lieutenant BM Bush DFC is pictured (right) with his navigator at Upwood in 1944.

Two 504 Squadron Hawker Hurricane Mk Is snapped at Castletown, Scotland, sometime between June 21st & September 2nd, 1940. A superb study of Battle of Britain aircraft, and again from 'Mike' Bush's personal album.

Again, although not a Battle of Britain incident, this snapshot from 'Mike' Bush's album shows a Spitfire Mk IIA of 66 Squadron after a landing accident at Exeter during the winter of 1940/41. Another squadron with a fine Battle of Britain record, the chances are that this Spitfire is also a veteran of 1940's air battles.

During less hectic times, crashed aircraft on airfields inevitably became the subject for enthusiastic amateur photographers. This 234 Squadron Spitfire was captured on film at St Eval in Cornwall, having crashed on October 9th, 1940. The pilot, Sergeant CH Bell, had destroyed a Do 17 off Newquay and was fortunately unhurt. Ultimately, however, Bell was reported Missing in 1941 and has no known grave.

Aircraft production was obviously of vital importance in 1940 and heavy raids were made against targets connected with the British aircraft industry. These Spitfires are seen under construction at the Supermarine factory at Woolston near Southampton.

On September 26th, 1940, KG55 attacked the Woolston works and caused great damage, as indicated by this photograph. Fortunately Spitfire production had already been dispersed, so that not all assemblies were undertaken under one roof. Furthermore, the shadow factory at Castle Bromwich was up and running, producing the Spitfire Mk II in numbers. For those reasons and because the raid came too late in the Battle of Britain, this German success had little or no effect on the outcome.

The Chief Test Pilot at the Castle Bromwich Aircraft Factory was the distinguished, record breaking, airman Alex Henshaw, seen here talking to the Prime Minister. At the time of writing Alex remains heavily involved in the Spitfire interest and is a member of both the Spitfire Society and Battle of Britain Historical Society.

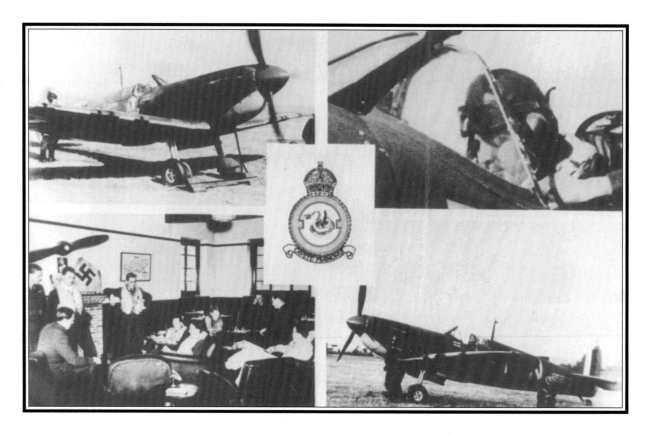

A postcard produced by 66 'Clickety-Click' Squadron at Gravesend during the Battle of Britain. The pilots are in the Watch Office – I wonder what happened to their trophies? Fourth from right, to the left of the chess table, is the author 'Dizzy' Allen DFC. The pilot in the 'office' is Flight Lieutenant Ken Gillies who commanded 'A' Flight between September 7th and the date he was reported Missing: October 4th. A successful fighter pilot, appropriately his son, John, organised the first ever post-war 66 Squadron reunion.

A knight and his steed: Flying Officer Thomas Smart of 65 'East India' Squadron with 'YT-T'. Having scored a number of victories over Dunkirk and during the Battle of Britain, Smart was awarded the DFC in 1941, followed by a Bar with effect from 1943. Sadly he did not survive the war, being killed flying Spitfires from Malta.

Sergeant Ron Stillwell DFM, again of 65 Squadron, prepares to take-off in 'YT-X'. Ron was also a successful fighter pilot who later commanded 65 Squadron whilst the unit operated Mustangs, during which time he was also awarded the DFC. Squadron Leader Stillwell was one of my earliest correspondents; sadly no longer with us he remains sorely missed.

Where the estate agent's sign came from I couldn't even hazard a guess! An interesting line up of 65 Squadron pilots taken after the Battle of Britain at RAF Tangmere: Sergeant Victor Lowson (a replacement pilot), Sergeant Ron Stillwell, Flying Officer Tommy Smart, Squadron Leader GAW Saunders, Pilot Officer Robin Norwood and Flying Officer Brendan Finucane. The latter became one of Fighter Command's most successful pilots during the first half of the war, but was sadly reported 'Missing' on July 15th, 1942. Wing Commander Finucane DSO, DFC** was 21-years old.

Pilot Officer RKC Norwood of 65 Squadron, whose father won the Victoria Cross whilst flying with the RFC during the Great War. After the Battle of Britain he became an instructor before joining 54 Squadron which was bound for the Middle East. Diverted to Australia, 54 Squadron flew Spitfires from Melbourne against the Japanese. Flight Lieutenant Norwood survived the war but died in 1970.

An interesting photograph believed taken on February 26th, 1941, when 616 Squadron relieved 65 Squadron at Tangmere. From left: unknown, Pilot Officer Jack Strang (NZ, a post-Battle of Britain replacement on 65 Squadron), Flying Officer Tommy Smart (65), unknown with pipe (but could this perhaps be Pilot Officer JE 'Johnnie' Johnson of 616?), Flying Officer Paddy Finucane (65), unknown.

Pilots of 66 Squadron's 'A' Flight at Exeter early in 1941. Battle of Britain pilots amongst them are Sergeant DAC Hunt (second left), Sergeant DCO Campbell (third left), and Sergeant WJ Corbin (extreme right). The photograph was taken by Battle of Britain veteran Pilot Officer LW 'Duke' Collingridge. The Spitfire is another presented by the Belfast Telegraph, P7843: 'Aldergrove'.

The next eight photographs appear courtesy of Squadron Leader RA Beardsley DFC, whose personal collection of 41 Squadron related photographs from 1940/41 can only be described as awesome. Bob lent me his collection to copy and use accordingly several years ago and I consider this to be an enormous privilege. Here Bob is pictured in his 'personal' Spitfire, 'EB-B'.

Battle of Britain pilots Sergeants Terry Healey and Bob Beardsley (second and extreme right respectively), pictured with two replacement 41 Squadron pilots at Hornchurch towards the end of 1940.

The all-important guns: Sergeant Terry Healey confers with Corporal Nunn as his Spitfire is re-armed at Hornchurch during September, 1940.

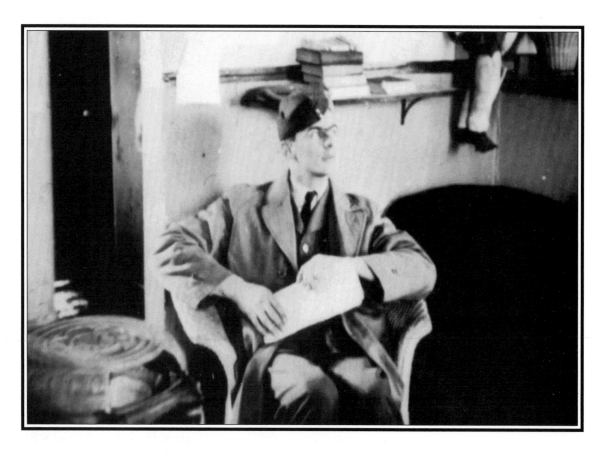

During the Battle of Britain, the 'Kiwi' Pilot Officer EP 'Hawkeye' Wells flew Spitfires with 266 & 41 Squadrons. Bob has pictured him here at Hornchurch during 1940. Wells was an extremely successful fighter pilot, safely concluding his war with 12 enemy aircraft destroyed, four probables, six and one shared damaged and another destroyed on the ground. An impressive tally by any standards.

Sergeants Beardsley, Mitchell and Usmar of 41 Squadron pictured at Catterick early in 1941. On September 27th, 1940, Frank Usmar was shot down over Kent; baling out, like James Coward, he only stopped himself bleeding to death by applying his wireless lead as a tourniquet to his right leg. This incident also emphasises what it meant to fight over your homeland: Usmar's home was in West Malling from where his parents actually watched him float to earth, blissfully unaware of the pilot's identity.

Squadron Leader DO Finlay DFC, 41 Squadron's CO. A former Olympic gold medallist, Finlay was a fitness fanatic who imposed a strict and physical regime upon his pilots. Retiring from the RAF in 1969, it is understood that the Group Captain took his own life in 1970 whilst suffering from depression. What a tragedy.

Pilot Officer AL 'Archie' Winskill, also of 41 Squadron. On August 14th, 1941, Winskill was shot down over France but made a 'Home Run'. He later flew with distinction over the Middle East and survived the war. Having remained in the post war RAF, he is now Air Commodore Sir 'Archie' Winskill and for several years commanded the Queen's Flight.

The final photograph from Squadron Leader Beardsley's album shows three Battle of Britain pilots whilst serving with 41 Squadron at Tangmere (Merston) in 1941: Flight Lieutenant Roy Bush DFC (a New Zealander who flew with 242 Squadron during the Battle of Britain), Squadron Leader Lionel Gaunce DFC (615 Squadron in 1940), and Flight Lieutenant Roy Marples DFC (616). Only Bush survived the war but was sadly killed in a flying accident during 1948.

The next six photographs come from the personal album of my old friend, the now late Flight Lieutenant HRG Poulton DFC who sadly died in 1998. Bob was also a VR pilot, and is pictured here at left at No 1 Initial Training Wing, Cambridge, in 1939. The other two pilots are, from left, Sergeant JE 'Johnnie' Johnson, later to become the RAF's top scoring fighter pilot of World War Two, and Sergeant PH Fox. All three survived the war and, I am privileged to say, have been involved in my various projects.

Bob Poulton pictured several years later when a battle hardened flight commander on 611 Squadron. Note the open top button and DFC diagonal ribbon.

Three 74 'Tiger' Squadron pilots snapped at Hornchurch during early 1941. Although the pilot at left is unknown, in the centre is the Polish Pilot Officer Henryk Szczesny, and at left is Pilot Officer Tony Bartley. Both named pilots survived the war, Bartley at one time being married to the famous British movie star Deborah Kerr.

More 'Tigers' at Hornchurch: Flight Lieutenant John Mungo-Park DFC, Flying Officer Roger Boulding, Squadron Leader CA Woods, next two unknown, Pilot Officer Bob Poulton.

No. 74 SQUADRON

Farewell Hot Pot

To WING COMMANDER

A. G. MALAN, D.S.O., D.F.C.

HELD AT . . .
"YE OLDE CHARLES" HOTEL
CLIFTONVILLE
FRIDAY . . APRIL 4th . . 1941

(and opposite) 74 Squadron's leader was that legendary South African, Adolf Guysbert 'Sailor' Malan. When promoted to lead the Biggin Hill Wing, the 'Tigers' held a farewell party. This is the menu, preserved all these years by Bob Poulton. There can be no doubt that a good time was had by all!

Toasts _____

1 THE KING

2 THE RETIRING
   COMMANDING OFFICER

        Proposed by
        S/Ldr. MUNGO PARK, D.F.C.

3 PRESENTATION

4 REPLY BY
   Wing-Commander
            A. G. MALAN, D.S.O., D.F.C.

5 OUR GUESTS
        Proposed by S/Ldr. C. A. WOOD

6 REPLY BY
   Wing-Commander G. BANNISTER

_____ _Menu_

HORS D'OEUVRES

.

BEER

.

THE HOT POT
WINE . HOCK

.

MORE BEER

.

THE SAVOURY

.

STILL MORE BEER

.

PORT

Don Kingal
HORNCHURCH JAN 1943.
122 SQUADRON

Another pilot to have flown 'my' Spitfire, R6644, was Don Kingaby, pictured here at Hornchurch whilst commanding 122 Squadron during 1943. Fighting with 92 Squadron at Biggin Hill throughout the Battle of Britain, his combat record not only earned him the title of '109 Specialist' but also the DFM and two Bars. As ever, although the pilot is identifiable the 'erk' remains anonymous.

The 'Wizard Midget': Flight Lieutenant Ian 'Widge' Gleed, of 87 Squadron, pictured at Exeter during the Battle of Britain. Another successful fighter pilot and leader, Gleed was to perish over the Middle East in 1943.

Although an oft used photograph, what a terrific image this is: Flight Lieutenant Gleed, in P2798, en route from Exeter to Bibury in Gloucestershire, August 1940. Flying Officer RF Watson took the snap from the cockpit of his own Hurricane.

A sobering image for those who dream of derring do: all that was left of Flying Officer Arthur Gowers' 85 Squadron Hurricane (V7343) on September 1st, 1940. The aircraft crashed at Star Lane, Hooley, near Redhill in Kent behind a C2 Billet. Fortunately the pilot baled out safely, albeit badly burnt, landing at Woldingham.

Credit: Colin Brown

Another snapshot from the album of 'Mike' Bush showing a 66 Squadron Spitfire damaged by the *Luftwaffe* during a night raid on Exeter in February, 1941. During the Battle of Britain this aircraft was the personal mount of 234 Squadron's top scoring pilot, Flying Officer Bob Doe ('AZ-D'). It finally perished in a fatal flying accident in Gloucestershire.

Hurricane pilot: Sergeant Laurence 'Rubber' Thorogood of 87 Squadron, Bibury 1940. Squadron Leader Thorogood DFC RAF (Retd), as he now is, appeared on the cover of my original 'Kaleidoscope' published in 1999. Volume III features a number of previously unpublished photographs from this pilot's personal album.

After the Battle of Britain a morale-boosting film was made about RJ Mitchell and the Spitfire's creation. Entitled 'The First of the Few' it was filmed at Ibsley and the cast included a number of actual Battle of Britain pilots. Here the stars, Leslie Howard (left) and David Niven (right) are pictured with a real hero: Squadron Leader Frank Howell DFC, at that time commanding 118 Squadron but in 1940 a flight commander with 609.

That's the spirit! 152 Squadron's groundcrew at Warmwell, summer 1940.

Ray Johnson was an armourer on 152 Squadron throughout virtually the whole war. He has taken the time and trouble to make a superb verbal record of his experiences by simply talking into a tape recorder. If only other survivors would follow his example!

Flying Officer Graham Cox, from Sparkhill in Birmingham, flew Spitfires with 152 Squadron and recorded several victories during the Battle of Britain. He later flew with distinction over both Malta and Italy, receiving both the DSO and DFC before leaving the RAF in 1946. He is pictured here at Warmwell in August, 1940.

Credit: Allan White

Hawker Hurricane test pilot Flight Lieutenant RC 'Dick' Reynell pictured (left) at the Brussels air show in July, 1939. He was killed on September 7th, 1940, along with fellow outstanding 43 Squadron pilot Flight Lieutenant Caesar Hull DFC (right). Reynell is buried at the Brookwood Military Cemetery in Surrey whilst Hull's grave can be found in Tangmere churchyard.

The next six photographs give some indication of the historian's common frustration. Frequently have I discovered albums in which photographs are un-captioned, the owner's memory being insufficient to assist with identifying

certain faces. This picture, from Bob Poulton's album, shows himself at right with Sergeant Denis 'Red' Parker at left during training, 1939. Who is the pilot in the middle?

Similar scenario from Pilot Officer Jack Hamar DFC's personal effects: he is pictured awaiting flight at left, who are the other two? Circa 1938.

Unknown pilot of 19 Squadron, believed late 1940 – early 1941.

From Bob Poulton's album, do these two photographs show the same Sergeant-Pilot, believed of 64 Squadron circa 1940?

Another from Bob Poulton, great study of a 92 Squadron Pilot or Flying Officer at Biggin Hill during the Battle of Britain, identity unknown!

222 'Natal' Squadron stalwart Sergeant Iain Hutchinson, who destroyed several Me 109s during the Battle of Britain.

Squadron Leader Hutchinson survived the war, retiring from the RAF in 1957. He has been a most welcome guest at several of our events and is pictured here at the launch of *Through Peril to the Stars*, Malvern, September 1993.

A 222 Squadron pilot who sadly did not survive the Battle of Britain was Flying Officer John Cutts. Shot down on September 4th, 1940, his Spitfire, X4278, crashed and burnt out at Amberfield Farm, Chart Sutton in Kent.

Due to the perhaps understandable administrative confusion at the time, Flying Officer Cutts, in Plot W143, became one of two 'Unknown Airmen' buried at Bell Road Cemetery, Sittingbourne. Having submitted conclusive evidence to the MOD during the course of research for my *Missing in Action: Resting in Peace?* (Ramrod Publications, 1998), the identity of both airmen was established. Consequently the Commonwealth War Graves Commission erected named headstones accordingly in 1999. This represented quite a personal triumph.

Safely home: 504 Squadron Hurricane about to touch down at Castletown, summer, 1940.

Another welcome guest at our events is Wing Commander CF 'Bunny' Currant DSO DFC* who flew Hurricanes with 605 'County of Warwick' Squadron in 1940 and rapidly accumulated an impressive score. In the wartime snap 'Bunny' is pictured whilst commanding 501 Squadron, more recently at the launch of my *Through Peril to the Stars* (Ramrod Publications, 1993).

Group Captain AB 'Woody' Woodhall, the Station Commander and 'Boss' Controller at Duxford during the Battle of Britain (pictured here in September, 1955). A close friend of Douglas Bader's and keen supporter of the Big Wing concept, Woodhall was a most colourful character who later served with distinction in Malta. During my research for *Bader's Duxford Fighters: The Big Wing Controversy* (Ramrod Publications, 1997) it was revealed in the 310 Squadron Operations Record Book that Woodhall had actually led the Squadron on patrol. This means that he is entitled to the Battle of Britain Clasp to the 1939-45 Star. Having provided the evidence to Wing Commander John Young, the Battle of Britain Fighter Association's historian, I look forward enormously to hearing that Group Captain Woodhall's name has been added to those of the Few. In 1941, in fact, Woodhall was Station Commander at Tangmere, where he and Douglas Bader teamed up once more, and during this time he even flew a Spitfire in several 'Circus' operations over enemy occupied France!

Another frequent guest of Ramrod Publications is Flight Lieutenant Geoffrey Stevens who flew Hurricanes with 213 Squadron from Tangmere in 1940. Pictured here at left during training, again the other pilot is unknown.

Like many other Battle of Britain survivors, Geoffrey Stevens later found himself flying over the Middle East. Here he is seen in a rare air-to-air snapshot of a tropical Hurricane.

After the Battle of Britain, other survivors would become prisoners of war, amongst them Sergeant Peter Ward-Smith of 610 Squadron who was shot down over France and captured on July 10th, 1941.

Incidents of 'Friendly Fire' in wartime air combat interest me very much, for a variety of reasons. Records indicate that on October 7th, 1940, Pilot Officer Dennis Adams of 611 Squadron was shot down by return fire from a Do 17 near Folkestone. In 1990, however, he explained to me that 'we had a new boy flying as Number Three who was trying to get himself a squirt. As I turned to attack he let fly and took out my controls plus half the instruments, and also put bullets in the fuel tank. I had quite a talk with this young man the following morning!' Dennis is pictured here at Digby in late 1939. Note the early aerial and lack of both an armoured windscreen and a rear-view mirror.

The Poles rapidly developed a reputation for determined ferocity during the air battles over England in 1940. This is Pilot Officer Gustav Radwanski who flew Hurricanes with 56 Squadron. Whilst flying Spitfires from Northolt in 1942 he lost

an arm in a mid-air collision. Unperturbed he became an instructor but returned to operational flying on Mustangs in 1945.

Pilot Officer Stefan Witorzenc flew Hurricanes with 501 Squadron and survived the war a distinguished Polish Wing Leader.

Sergeant Frank Twitchett joined 43 Squadron in the north of England in September, 1940, before moving to 229 Squadron at Northolt in October. He survived the Battle of Britain unscathed but had a close call with 145 Squadron in 1941 when his Spitfire was badly damaged by an Me 109 over France. After the war, Frank remained in the RAF until 1950. Between 1966-1972 he instructed the ATC on Chipmunks.

Flight Lieutenant Frank Twitchett was another most welcome and regular guest at Ramrod Publications' various events. He is pictured here at our 'Battle of Britain Day 1998' symposium, held at Worcester Guildhall in November that year, with aviation poet Larry McHale. Tragically Frank died suddenly the following week and remains much missed by us all.

Photograph courtesy Worcester Evening News.

Certain members of the august Battle of Britain Fighter Association pictured at Alconbury in 1987. Sadly many of these men have since departed, including Squadron Leader James 'Ginger' Lacey, one of Fighter Command's genuinely most successful fighter pilots in 1940 (pictured at extreme left of those sitting on the floor). These modest gentlemen, without whose courage and tenacity the British way of life would have perished 60 years ago, have sought little or no recognition for either themselves or their great achievement.

Others, however, myself included, feel passionately that the Few should be recognised and, indeed, their victory remembered. The Battle of Britain Historical Society, for example, has been instrumental in persuading Westminster City Council to provide an appropriate site for a Battle of Britain Monument in London. My role has been to work alongside the chosen sculptor, Kenneth Potts ARBS, to produce several ideas for consideration. The first two of these were unveiled at the original 'Kaleidoscope's' launch at the IWM Duxford Airfield on September 12th, 1999. Here Squadron Leader Laurence Thorogood DFC and Lady Bader do the honours.

A second unveiling took place at Worcester Guildhall at our book signing there on October 9th, 1999. Pictured with both maquettes are (* indicates one of the Few): Wing Commander John Freeborn DFC*, Mr Fred Roberts, Mr Peter Fox*, aviation poet Larry McHale, sculptor Kenneth Potts, Dr Gordon Mitchell, Mr Ernest French, Flight Lieutenants Gordon Batt*, Ken Wilkinson* and Richard Jones*, the author & publisher Dilip Sarkar, Flight Lieutenant Keith Lawrence DFC*, Mr Bob Morris and Mr Bill Kirk. Just out of frame was Miss Margaret Balfour.

It is hoped that the 60th anniversary year will see the London Monument Appeal gather in momentum and achieve popular support. Let us leave this book with a sobering thought: nearly 3,000 airmen qualified for the Battle of Britain Clasp, 544 of which actually gave their lives during the battle; many others had perished, however, by 1945, some many miles from home. This is the grave of one of them, Flight Sergeant Peter Mitchell who flew Spitfires during the Battle of Britain with 65 Squadron. He was killed on July 26th, 1942, whilst serving in India with 79 Squadron. The 20-year old's grave can be found in Bhowanipore Cemetery, Calcutta.

Author's Postscript

Although born 21-years after the Battle of Britain was fought, it concerns me greatly that despite the significance of this particular victory the summer of 1940 has recently appeared in danger of drifting into obscurity, forgotten by the masses. To emphasise this point I would use but one story. In July 1999, a local primary school teacher invited me to talk to some older children about the Second World War. To my astonishment, however, I discovered that not only had the children never heard of the Battle of Britain but neither had the teacher. What was more disturbing is that the lady in question was not a youngster but both mature and experienced.

Over the years I have been involved with numerous commemorative projects, such as memorials, exhibitions and publications, aimed at increasing awareness of the Battle of Britain. From the outset, back in the mid-1980s, our idea was not to merely exhibit at aviation museums, and arguably in the process preach merely to the already converted, but to bring the Battle of Britain to the high street and in so doing increase the general public's awareness and appreciation. The success of this concept was proven through attendance figures at our exhibitions, including, for example, the 10,000 visitors in four months who enjoyed our 'Spitfire!' exhibition at Tudor House Museum in Worcester. Furthermore, in 1990, our 50th anniversary of the Battle of Britain commemorative exhibition attracted a staggering 18,000 visitors in six months. Clearly provided interest is either reawakened or freshly stimulated, the Battle of Britain continues to inspire.

From the outset of my publishing career back in May 1990, when my first book *Spitfire Squadron* (Air Research Publications, 1990) was launched at the RAF Battle of Britain Museum, Hendon, we adopted an inter-active approach to publishing. At that and subsequent launches to mark the release of my 10 further titles, we have assembled numerous of the Few, their support staff and associated personalities. Most welcome guests over the years have included, for example, Lady Dowding, Lady Bader, Gulf War POW John Peters, Dr Gordon Mitchell, AVM JE Johnson and, indeed, German pilots. These events have given both enthusiasts and the general public a unique opportunity to actually meet personalities from the pages of history books. Naturally it has been both a dream come true and an enormous privilege to have personally been instrumental in providing this rich experience.

As most enthusiasts will know, many of the surviving Few are members of the Battle of Britain Fighter Association. When writing the original 'Kaleidoscope' in 1999, my information was that the Association intended to wind up this year, due to the members' advancing age and diminishing numbers. It gives me enormous pleasure to report, however, that this is not actually the case, as the Association intends to continue beyond this 60th anniversary year. This really is tremendous news as I have always felt strongly that the Association should exist until such time as the Few become naturally extinct. When that sad but ultimately inevitably time comes, all of the Few can be assured of one thing:-

We *Will* Remember Them

THE DOUGLAS BADER FOUNDATION

S ir Douglas Bader was a legend in his own lifetime. He led from the front not just as a war hero but also as a disabled person. He lived life by his own philosophy that "a disabled person who fights back is not handicapped.....he is inspired".

Following his untimely death the Douglas Bader Foundation was established to continue his inspirational work in true Bader spirit. Although the Foundation is but a small charity it has set itself considerable targets replicating the characteristics of Douglas Bader in advancing and developing its support work amongst the disabled community.

Since the successful completion of phase 1 of its work, the opening in 1993 of The Douglas Bader Centre at Roehampton, further initiatives have been launched by the Foundation. These include the introduction of The Douglas Bader Grant Scheme, a support programme designed to assist those with disabilities in overcoming their difficulties in the pursuance of achievement. More recently, the introduction of BADERline *(0845 609 1919)*, a telephone helpline specifically for amputee disabled, their families and supporters has started to make an impact and is already attracting a large number of users.

The name of Douglas Bader, all he stood for and the continued development of his innovative work amongst the disabled community needs everyone's support. YOU CAN HELP us to help them by making a contribution either by donation, legacy or covenant to:-

THE DOUGLAS BADER FOUNDATION
The Douglas Bader Centre, Roehampton Lane,
London. SW15 5DZ.
Tel: 0181 788 1551 - Fax: 0181 789 5622
Email : douglasbaderfdnbtinternet. com

REMEMBER........*"A disabled person who fights back is not handicapped....................he is inspired".*

Sir Douglas Bader

Charity Registration No 800435

138